PLEASE HOLD

poems

PLEASE HOLD

poems

by
Muriel Nelson

Encircle Publications, LLC
Farmington, Maine USA

Please Hold ©2021 Muriel Nelson

Paperback ISBN-13: 978-1-64599-177-9
Kindle ISBN-13: 978-1-64599-178-6

All rights reserved. No part of this book may be reproduced in any form by any mechanical or electronic means including storage and retrieval systems without express written permission in writing from the publisher. Brief passages may be quoted in review. Rights to individual poems remain with the author.

Editor: Cynthia Brackett-Vincent
Book and book cover design: Eddie Vincent/ENC Graphics Services
Cover Image: Shutterstock.com

Sign up for Encircle Publications newsletter and specials
http://eepurl.com/cs8taP

Printing: Walch Publishing, Portland, Maine

Mail Orders, Author Inquiries:
Encircle Publications
PO Box 187
Farmington, ME USA 04938
207-778-0467

Online orders:
encirclepub.com

Acknowledgements
with gratitude

Poems in this collection first appeared in the following publications:

88: A Journal of Contemporary American Poetry:
"Gargoyle's Ankyloglossia"

The Antigonish Review:
"A woman with a hole in her brain the size of a lemon says"

Beloit Poetry Journal: "For the Night People" and
"To Wit, To Dote"

bosque literary journal: "Rumor's a Fun Fact"

Canary: "Rumor's a Fun Fact" (republication)

Heliotrope: "In a Whisper"

Memorious: "Mister Death"

The National Poetry Review: "Nap"

New American Writing: "A Kind of Doting" and
"Sonnet on Air"

Northwest Review: "Gargoyle's Undoings"

Penumbra: "You There"

Snake Nation Review: "Up to You"

Superstition Review: "Hold Sway"

The voices of generous souls inspire and accompany the best of my work. I'm especially grateful to Patricia Corbus, Martha Zweig, Eleanor Wilner, Heather McHugh, Dean Young, and Lee Sharkey for the sparks their comments have ignited in these poems. I'm grateful as well to Cynthia Brackett-Vincent for her sharp eye and able editing. My heartfelt thanks go to many others whose friendship and creative spirits have shaped my poems over time: alumni and mentors of the MFA Program for Writers at Warren Wilson and several writers' conferences, former colleagues at Pierce and Highline Colleges, the Northwest Renaissance, the GGs, musicians in choral and instrumental ensembles, and my first workshop buddies Jeanne Matthews and Bill Reed.

Dedication

To you word lovers with lives on hold
who hold this book and long to hold the lives you love—

To essential workers
who keep us all alive—

And especially to Jim, Evan, Ryan, Anne-Julienne, and Dan
who keep *the* (and me) *alive*

Table of Contents

In a Whisper 1
Sonnet on Air 2
A Few Words from a Haystack with Facehole 3
Clear Air Turbulence 4
Rumor's a Fun Fact 5
Up to You 6
Virtuoso Dreamer Whispers to the Dead 7
Fear, the great toucher 8
Gargoyle's Ankyloglossia 9
Gargoyle's Undoings 10
From a Heretic's Hermitage 11
Nap 12
Mister Death 13
Second Story Window 14
Life Force 15
God Deafness 16
You There 17
A woman with a hole in her brain the size of a lemon says . 18
Hold Sway 19
A Kind of Doting 20
The myth of mountains 22
Hug 23
The Alive 24
For the Night People 25
To Wit, To Dote 26

About the Author 28

In a Whisper

This is just a hug.
And a kiss on the cheek.
They do it all the time—*don't jump*—
Someone's watching.
There's no smoke, no mark
that will show. It's nothing.
Now go . . .

Sonnet on Air

That leap in the shape of a lean cat,
that sun-fired kerfuffle of things with feathers,
that puff of lost patience now rising it seems
from a fencepost or maybe a sparrowhawk,
do these matter? *Are* they matter?
This writing on air with its N_2s and O_2s,
its chemical Scrabble, the whole composition,
will it save? Be saved?
Eighty-something Bruce flies on his skis.
He says only motion and cognition matter.
Eighty-something Max landed wrong off her horse
but still lands sharp word-claws right *here*.
The lifts they give us in the shape of a wing, our steaming, our rising,
will these alter weather forever? Or like contrails, disappear?

A Few Words from a Haystack with Facehole

Words like worms wriggle out when it rains
the slow kind of rain, rain turning white
trying to rise from falling to flying for a moment
but going to pieces on the ground. Lovely
pieces and words broken for everyone
like *Jesus the (Any)way, soothing sooth*,
or *hapsichord*'s broken chords played wrong
the way holes in clothes are wrong unless they're
lace holes, the way pasta and sauce or loaves
and fish never come out even, so you add
to one or the other and eat forever,
or the way a dog learns daylight savings
time in no time and gets you up early
with *I have to go to go to go*,
and then shows you noses you shows you each place
where someone or something mysterious has been
and right *there* where the super worm moon is setting.
Your head starts to play an old song of your dad's,
By the light (by the light) of the super worm moon,
silvery womb, or something, *I love...*
that you haven't missed bird breakfast. See, the birds
have sprung forward as worms crawl out, but the world
everywhere stays dark. Over there, shadows
are moving against orange house holes, but here
you've gone a bit crazy, it seems, sequestered.
Your head, that haystack, hasn't been out
for a haircut or anything else. What it hears
on the radio are probably lies—how few
are ill and have died, *according to*—what?—
my reporting. But how is everyone? Today's whole
truth. Please. The voice stumbles, *We certainly*
(pause) *don't know*. Is there time? *We don't know.*

Clear Air Turbulence

From the window, a cat studies flight
while a veil I dared to take
from a chest flies from the berries
it's supposed to protect. The cat quivers.
Teeth chatter as a crow swoops down.
White flutters. Currants take their time.
Take a breath. Say *anima*.
Now you've said it twice.

CAT is a mystery still.
No clue, no white cloud of nature's
underside—flight's camouflage,
cat's belly—or bride's slow-walk hide
when out of the see-forever clear
comes the pilot's pale fear and the wife's.
That troubled air. It takes
your veil, your breath, your life.

Rumor's a Fun Fact

Roofs are steaming like beekeepers' smokers,
or a roof is burning while bees smoke.
Plum petals fall so snowingly
that rain doesn't show,
and my old foe photinia
votes again for the red party
blocking out windows with leaflets.
It's peaceful, though, isn't it?
The president's people say *everyone knows*
whatever they claim today. Now
they say the president's making good
(on one of his threats).
Others say a mustache is making war.
It's shady business, so here come the pines
where there's just enough room for a chair
between our old rhododendron
and new burning bush
if you'd care to sit
as crowds re-enact Exodus and sicken.
The air is as still as on 9/11,
the bees so calm you can hold
a tasting in the bloom by your arm
but not a loved one nearby,
or watch an ant rick-racking rough wood
while it climbs an inch or two as if, *as if*
(*as if* could take us anywhere),
as if bees weren't endangered,
as if there were no drought coming,
no virus, and no threat of smoke in the still air.
As if this too-early warmth with its plain blue sky,
green burning bush, and huge, gentle blossoms were normal,
were good.

Up to You

What quakes here
among other things, are alder or aspen,
fullness like squirrels' tails (bone trembling through),
gold and brown dapple made partial, detached,
gold leaf down brown water, brown spot down gold leaf.

Then the low, hard sun—*I won't get carried away*—suddenly
blues this puddle and storms it all to high heaven.

Virtuoso Dreamer Whispers to the Dead

Let's conspire.
While Bach sleeps and you're enskyed
slip Legos into his hands
so we can *see* him build his fantasies,
his spirit level bubbling by
with hummingbirds, those stained glass counters
pointing in and out of 1-2-3-4 flowers,
flashing ruby throats and wingspeed. Quick!
Some variations while the moment lasts!
Bach's record is three themes at once. Raise him?
The birds count up tomato futures as they
counterpoint borage and honeysuckle. Higher?
Yellows, blues, and pinks are all in motion while
your favorite retrograde's brought heat before the fire
wood's been planted. Copper hair is flaming fro and fro
as anger afterimages ghost green to light
the north, then touch and go, touch and fly
off again where all that doesn't matter isn't.
Take me there! (before I wake)
I hear a teacher yelling, 'Nail the white,'
to kill his scribbling students' time.
Stop it! Clouds here are forever
turning mountains into molehills.
A break of sun,
crack of earth,
spurt of steam—
and molehills reach the sky.

Fear, the great toucher

blows cold down your back
and thumbs glissandos
up your bone xylophone.
A bear paw inside your tent
comes *this* close to you,
the only one awake to shiver.
Your phone at home
reaches out to ice your ear—
*We know things. We know
you're at risk unless you act.*
Your doors are all locked, yet
dry fingers brush your neck.
It could be, you whisper, *it could
and you could be blamed.*
You're this goat, that goat,
subjunctives gone wild.
Now hooves pound your chest.
It's true. Your fear is a fact.

Gargoyle's Ankyloglossia

Caught
open-mouthed between fearful and fierce,

a stone alone,
outcast, lives

like a cat who's finished screaming
and stiffens, electrified.

One move,
just a twitch, might rub up the charge.

A whole gesture toward
you now could go wrong.

Curses, prayers and exhaust rise outdoors
like steam. Who can distinguish them,
jumbled on streets where lights are still long?

What if
from the ugliest mouth on the corner, love stuck
out its bent lightning tongue?

Gargoyle's Undoings

Don't say, somebody says
and the *don't say* grows on the tongue's tip like gristle.

Don't touch, you say to yourself
and your touched shadow lengthens to stain a wall.

You could bumble right into it—anyone could—
moved by who knows what,

maybe nothing at all.

So there you are: out of shape, headlong,
mouth shadowed (whose doesn't matter) by mouth,
breath shadowed (whose is air?) by breath—
while seeds turn to birdthings—fluted liquid—
flutist's belly to watermelon (mouth pursed for seeds).
Thump hard, said the flutist, *as hard as you can.* (I couldn't.)

But O Most Shy,

if I happen to glimpse your
bellows and gasp, catching your far-flung breath

like a baby breathing perfectly
(at last)—don't stop

my tongue. Let me breathe out again. Don't
close my eye.

From a Heretic's Hermitage

It's Lent, but I haven't given up
anything for certain for Lent
for I love fish. Forgive me.

It's spring, but I haven't considered the ant
as it labors to carry aphids underground to milk them,
and up again to feed on green gardens—ours!

I do consider two crows who are nesting as usual.
One watches our cat and me while the other,
in a single swoop, breaks off a twig, poops, and flies.

Now our bathroom scale, priestly beast, preaches
on laying up for myself weighty treasures.
It adds by tens, taunts *ERR—ERR*, and grades me *00*.

All the days of my life I've piled up things to repair.
Ruins have charm, for sure, but whoever
says, *I want to be a ruin when I grow up?*

Oh, happy is the woman whose perfume is coffee, a believer
whose family and friends still write, talk, and breathe,
and who finds when she digs in dirt now, that it's warm

and worms aren't
the least bit
interested in her.

Nap

    after Antonio Machado

While internal combustion hums
and hos, brains storm and turbulence roughens
flyways, black and blue wings mix up
casting seeds, and radios amplify hubbubs,
a truck spills mirrors. Heavens,
suns, yellow farms, and freeway go suddenly
daffy declaring kaleidoscope love.
Let us honor the Lord—his holy Narcissus,
sharp cut of his strong suit, his splitting image,
its cracks, piercings, toll, and its tollings.

God of great pain, lone,
self-bombing, bloody-crossed God, you let down wings
to nest your blue egg, and we crouch
here—we, your afters, dark afterimages, your tears.

You give sleep and deep sleep and deeper. . .
for our troubles, and arm us with lovers'
dreams, while your I Am I Am iambs beat you forever—
you whom no one hugs, you untouchable, sharp, broken One.

Mister Death

    after E. E. Cummings

who do you play with now
    you with your toy tonsils appendixes legs breasts

Hitler's
kaput
    who used the salute
    to collect for you

tapping toes to *Tristan*   one   million   two   million   three
                                                      Christ

kaput too?

oh they were all lovely handsome
    believable collectible breakablejustlikethat
            but what i want to know is

how do you like your blueeyed cancers
        your viruses

Mister Death
they won't die for you will they

Second Story Window

Oak force overfills each pane.
Greens deep-breathe. Such generosity

I can't see the ends of it.
I can't see what wind does with limbs,

only their unsolid sway as leaves hiss and, below
mist rolls like a broken wave's foam.

You die awake all night and grow
till God, who contours love with dark,

who forsakes even Christ, lifts brass bells
to burnish this trunk, and a shadow to sing.

Life Force

It's there. In the tansy. In the dandelion,
that little low sun. And brighter still,
one spot in that lawn long ago turned gray
from St. Helens' ash, soft as a fine
flannel suit with its perky boutonniere *alive*.
God's joke. God with solar-powered blooms.
Bulbs. Bugs. Up on the all-the-world's stage
failing to get a laugh (story of his eternity). Alone
as the man I once knew whose face couldn't smile.
The face of gray waters. Where jokes looked cruel.
Look now. God of the marigold, crocus, and daffodil,
hosting their gold, prefers weeds. Buttercups burgeon
with gloss for teasing and roots for invading. When we
fall sick, the teeter totters, and weeds inherit the earth.

God Deafness

I'm amazed
at that silent laughter
when the deaf world cries in high voices,
its most nasal of *vox humana*s seeking ear,
that very ear which the ancients sorely tried
in excessive rhyme (*Incline thine*)
in commands (*Keep me*)
and in begging (*Give*)
and which now we assault in the common curse.
I'm amazed
at that chuckle I couldn't hear
shaking my bed, my home, my universe.
That ultra-low purr,
is it your scary business? Your pleasure?

You There

No one mentions, here, that hummingbirds
buzz like balloons' loose lips,
that on stage, when bows flash and brasses tune,
the oboe's A could flat disappear,
or plants, faced south and left alone
on a sill, might wilt and bow to their sun.

Rather than dazzle, please mail juncos,
send out your A-440 to me, and (outside
our window) keep rain, which is hope.
There's enough smooth talk.
Finesse means finished.
I need pauses—to connect, go on.

Show me you're not all together
without me. It's blushes, squirms,
stumbles I live on (a flash'll
get panned), plus that hitch
you don't plan: in your voice,
it's a catch.

A woman with a hole in her brain the size of a lemon says

I find repetition soothing. Really?
Let me donate that woofer blaring its beats to her.
And Mark's souped-up Olds, its starter trying and trying,
then its growl when it comes back to life and smokes
up the street. Or a grating voice overheard in a store:
*I wish you would stop repeating over and over
and over. It's so repetitious, so redundant,
so cliché, so been there, done that. Bor-ing.*

Yet there are waves that could soothe me forever—
their rhythmic roar, their infinite angles on how
to come in. Our family's homecomings, called in or not,
time and times again. Your car's dark tracks
in ice-crusted snow as you back down our drive, turn onto
the street and pull forward drawing a graceful *seven*,
the hour you plan to be home, traffic and weather
permitting, when finally your headlights and crunching tires
complete a triangle, pleasing this engineer's daughter.
And the door you open, the door you shut and secure.
Your steps on the floor, keys in the drawer, and your breathing
later, your quiet breathing in sleep. So ordinary
it seems these will always soothe me at night as before.
Soothe me now once more.

Hold Sway

Afraid of height?
Of shifting logs?
Of the lone fir left at quitting time
or the perch a crow blackens? Never mind
the fir's wild sway, its scanty roots grown in crowded
woods. On the ground lie plenty of balance poles,
and around us, electrons, scientists say, push back.
There's wind to lean on now, that white-noise version
of crow song that's matched by the mind's ear's sibilance:
Fauré's sweeping *sanctus, sanctus* clears
another space. A violin tries its wings—
sanctus—lifts and circles back—then rises
over orange machines and trills through diesel
smoke as the crow flies to a higher place.

A Kind of Doting

Strange beings we are.
Baby facemakers
>playing the lifetime sport
>of peek-a-boo.

Verify, verify, we say
believing our peeks
>between cheaters' fingers. *Look!*
>*Everything's true*

(in wedges). How magical, then,
are fingers and eyelids.
>When they close, powers go free.
>Wonderful, too,

are weaknesses. Like mine
for strengths out of view—
>forces of tree candles, male cones,
>maidenhair ferns,

clear skies, seas, yeast.
Our fondness for bubbling
>in bread, egg whites, cream—
>the *air* we love

to eat. Dearer still
is the air we could breathe
>but not notice when we sang requiems
>and now, if under our breaths,

pain arrives like sunset
in cathedrals, unhurried,
> taking over, dismissing all worries
> like children—*Yes,*

you may go now, yes. Then black
as night-stained glass,
> pain looms. You try to slow
> your breaths while it finds

that place behind the eyelids
and grows in the dark.
> You endure. Then a stem appears—
> a live path—to a quiet iris.

The myth of mountains

is the oldest myth around here,
whispered all through the lowlands
and out to canoes in the sound
as the dew point reaches us over and over
transforming fog into something heard,
like the belief that music's always
beating inside each body waiting
for someone to make a move or open a mouth.
The God-in-the-mountain tale calms
when predictable waves of rain come *down*,
down from elsewhere, elsewhere invisible,
down with healing vibrations
that feel like being purred over
by some being pleased over being itself. Over being.

Hug

Ugly word.
Like *hag* or *hog*, but worse.
Sound of exhalation stopped. Swallowed. Ugh.
Still, it's better than 'up in arms'
or 'get your arms around this.'
A hug's not about arms at all, is it?
Should we say, I want a *front*? *Affront*? *Abreast*? *Vest*? *Invest*?
How about *waffle*? And say I want
powdered sugar blowing over everyone
in some Belgian town square. Everyone going *soft*
and crusty and sweet, and breathing in
the scent of baking, waves of breathing
you can feel in waffle sandwich celebrations.
The whole cobblestone square a waffle,
its powder snow *melting*.
Once an antique waffle iron (a *hug* maker!) grabbed
my attention. Actually it sat (on no hands)
on a woodstove in an iron frame with a ball joint
so that even a diminutive cook could lift its handle in one hand,
twirl the waffle-to-be like a dance partner, and set it down
where it's warm to bake the other side. Best of all, it shaped
each waffle *like a four-leafed clover, each leaf a heart*.
For some lucky bride. Over there's a wedding photo of Grandmother,
her solemn face, her tiny jacket with hand stitching *holding her shape*
right here in my room even now. And here's a snapshot of her mother
cheek-to-cheek with her horse. Of course, ancestors on lonely
homesteads didn't always wear finery, stifle coughs, hold
still, and sit straight side-by-side with spouses, not touching.
They're ancestors, for heaven's sake!
They *held each other*. They *waffled*.

The Alive

In the year you turned our forks tines up
everything changed. Doors shut and we ate alone,
hugged air and talked from squares. Gloves were in
and on, but not because tines were sharp.
Masks, too, plastic outfits, and the burka
made perfect sense. *The alive*, though, struggled—
muffled, vented, snuffed. Negative pressure saved
some *alive*s. Positive pressure saved others
or killed. *We don't want your air!* Your air—
that trouble, that treasure. Huge protests over breathing rose.
Don't touch, people said, and touch became stuff of dreams.
A dream hand with a pen burst out from a page
as somewhere a beak pierced its shell. A dream ball,
that spiked 'Morning Star' red as Mars, hovered and stuck
around. Two horseshoe magnets stuck together
when hands reached to hold someone sick, but touched
only glass where mirror hands were pressed.
That glass grew *warm*. We'll always have music,
we thought, song to bring words to life, but *no!*
No to super-spreader choirs. No to singing doctors at the end
of long shifts. Go to your rooms! Group singing kills.
Do we still have those words we saved in small boxes?
Messages in a cloud? Songs that came to us airless,
on airwaves? Poems that hold bright moments' shapes?
It's May again now, May of blooms
and St. Helens' ash, May of Memorial Day.
In a mysterious letter she hid away, Emily Dickinson
asks, *Have you the little chest—to put the alive—in?*
Which little chest? Your live one? Your coffin?
It's 'sweet May', spring-loaded May, hoping-
chest May, and the only end's a question,
Do we have what it takes to keep *the alive* in?

For the Night People

A little celebration:
it's six a.m. and we're not sick.

Each of your doors breathes peace. So far
(I'm testing morning) coffee obeys gravity's law.
Streetside, brakes screech as always: the paper's here. A bird
hits a pane, not hard, and our cat apparently sleeps.

I'm testing morning for you. The news mixes
protests, fires, president's lies, virus alive, small war
enlarged, cement truck overturned on the Narrows Bridge with importance
of finding language for pain. There's a sheen on things. Names

shrink-wrap them for afterlives. There's no more
running for yours. On your lives, I'm swearing,
I say *guaranteeing* for life's time a little
celebration. For you,

did God die? (It's good to know when you love.) One
night, the "J" Writer scrolled back creation to dust.
Then mist. Next, a man-doll with uneven ribs, Eve,
and their God-potter all breathed.

Much later, our Apple ticked forever to say: *Carefully Saving*.
Strange—we kept things in Apples with glass eyes,
we who didn't know what to make of joys, we who can't help
but in morning make noise.

To Wit, To Dote

When the mind minds sometimes, then doesn't mind at all,
heart's boarded up, then downy-nested, opened wide,

is it that 'certain age' when trees take off their clothes for cold,
or spell when, feeling ill, they foolishly send all their buds?

Well, hello illness, I know you. You're the tiresome guy who stays
too long, drinks all the wine, and finally spins us dry. Anon.,

anon, I say: *Not I* soon enough. The garbage gods
will come collect. Will wit be wizened then, or I awake?

Will the alarm cat pounce in such a nick? Do you think? I hope.
I hope for purring, turbulence, for some god-bed vibrations.

But now (dear words), *but now*, this morning finds the vertical
to measure shorts and longs—short tenderness of autumn bud,

longing reach for blue which sounds cry's hues, gymnastics
in four-chambered pump, flappery of feathered thing,

limbs' wish to hold the whole outdoors in some fine doting spree
now, while inner space is lightened by a growing sense of sky.

Note

"Virtuoso Dreamer Whispers to the Dead": Hummingbirds may be able to count. A study conducted by Susan D. Healy, T. Andrew Hurly, Maria C. Tello-Ramos, and Tas I. F. Vámos and published by the Royal Society in July, 2020, found that rufous hummingbirds demonstrated "numerical ordinal abilities" which "could be used during foraging in the wild."

About The Author

Muriel Nelson's publications include *Part Song* (Bear Star Press, Dorothy Brunsman Poetry Prize) and *Most Wanted* (ByLine Press, ByLine Chapbook Award). Nominated five times for the Pushcart Prize, Nelson's poems have appeared in *Beloit Poetry Journal, Guesthouse, Hayden's Ferry Review, Hunger Mountain, New American Writing, Ploughshares, Smartish Pace*, and others, as well as in several anthologies. Two of her poems have been set to music. She holds master's degrees from the University of Illinois School of Music and the MFA Program for Writers at Warren Wilson College, and she lives with her husband in Federal Way, Washington. All her life she's enjoyed music and digging in dirt, most recently to challenge our political leaders and her small garden to do more for those who have less.

www.ingramcontent.com/pod-product-compliance
Lightning Source LLC
Chambersburg PA
CBHW021126080526
44587CB00010B/650